1 & 2 PETER
and JUDE

12 studies
for individuals or groups

Carolyn Nystrom

With Notes for Leaders

☙ Scripture Union is an international Christian charity working with churches in more than 130 countries providing resources to bring the good news about Jesus Christ to children, young people and families – and to encourage them to develop spiritually through the Bible and prayer. As well as coordinating a network of volunteers, staff and associates who run holidays, church-based events and school Christian groups, Scripture Union produces a wide range of publications and supports those who use their resources through training programmes.

Scripture Union, 207-209 Queensway, Bletchley, MK2 2EB, UK.
e-mail: info@scriptureunion.org.uk
www.scriptureunion.org.uk

Scripture Union Australia: Locked Bag 2, Central Coast Business Centre, NSW 2252.
www.su.org.au

ISBN 978 1 85999 753 6

First published in the United States by InterVarsity Press 1992, revised 2002.
Published in Great Britain by Scripture Union 2000. Reprinted 2003, 2004, 2005, 2007.

British Library Cataloguing-in-Publication data: a catalogue record for this book is available from the British Library.

Printed in Great Britain by goodmanbaylis, The Trinity Press, Worcester and London.

Contents

Getting the Most Out of
1 & 2 Peter and Jude

It was a shaky time for Christians in the Roman Empire. In A.D. 68 Emperor Nero saw himself surrounded by political enemies and took the easy way out: suicide. In the next year three emperors, in rapid succession, took his place but couldn't hold the job. So in A.D. 69 troops proclaimed the military leader Vespasian as emperor—and saw that he stayed there.

Vespasian hated Jews, and he counted Christians among them. Prior to becoming emperor his goal had been to trample Judea and erase it from existence. As emperor he sent his oldest son, Titus, to finish the job. Titus put Jerusalem under siege for three months. Then he tightened the noose. Troops leveled buildings to the ground. The temple became a crumble of stones. Jerusalem fell. Jews (and Christians) became Roman captives.

Aftershocks vibrated throughout the Roman Empire, blending with the general persecution against "atheists" (people who refused to worship Roman gods) that Nero had begun. Christians everywhere suffered. They were driven from their homes, deported to the outer borders of the empire, forbidden to worship openly and, worse yet, splintered by their own internal doctrinal disputes.

It is possible that the apostle Paul was martyred under Nero. And Peter was martyred as well—crucified upside down, tradition says, because he felt unworthy to die in the same position as his Lord. It was a dark season for Christians.

How were they to endure?

The Letters

Peter and Jude, through God's inspiration, sensed this coming darkness. If conservative scholars are correct, Peter's first letter can be dated about A.D. 64, probably written from the city of Rome—which Peter called Babylon in 5:13. Peter's second letter refers appreciatively in 3:15-16 to Paul's letters but bears no hint that Paul is dead. On the other hand, Peter seems to anticipate his own death—soon (see 2 Peter 1:13-14). Scholars therefore date this letter in the sixties as well—but closer to the end of the decade. Jude, the half-brother of Jesus Christ, wrote in the same era. In fact, much of the information in Jude is also found in 2 Peter 2. All three letters aim at preparing Christians for hardship.

But these are not bleak letters. Indeed they are full of hope and practical counsel on how to endure. They tell us to balance holy living with correct doctrine, to nurture spiritual growth, to work within existing authority structures and to take care of each other.

These letters do not tell us how to escape suffering but rather to expect it. They show us that in the midst of suffering we can enjoy our fellowship with other believers and look forward to a new heaven and a new earth, a "home of righteousness," with an end to pain.

These letters, sent with prophetic love to first-century Christians, still live today. They are a compass for our own dark road.

Suggestions for Individual Study

1. As you begin each study, pray that God will speak to you through his Word.

2. Read the introduction to the study and respond to the personal reflection question or exercise. This is designed to help you focus on God and on the theme of the study.

3. Each study deals with a particular passage—so that you can delve into the author's meaning in that context. Read and reread the passage to be studied. The questions are written using the language of the New International Version, so you may wish to use that version of the Bible. The New Revised Standard Version is also recommended.

4. This is an inductive Bible study, designed to help you discover for yourself what Scripture is saying. The study includes three types of questions. *Observation* questions ask about the basic facts: who, what, when, where and how. *Interpretation* questions delve into the meaning of the passage. *Application* questions help you discover the implications of the text for growing in Christ. These three keys unlock the treasures of Scripture.

Write your answers to the questions in the spaces provided or in a personal journal. Writing can bring clarity and deeper understanding of yourself and of God's Word.

5. It might be good to have a Bible dictionary handy. Use it to look up any unfamiliar words, names or places.

6. Use the prayer suggestion to guide you in thanking God for what you have learned and to pray about the applications that have come to mind.

7. You may want to go on to the suggestion under "Now or Later," or you may want to use that idea for your next study.

Suggestions for Members of a Group Study

1. Come to the study prepared. Follow the suggestions for individual study mentioned above. You will find that careful preparation will greatly enrich your time spent in group discussion.

2. Be willing to participate in the discussion. The leader of your group will not be lecturing. Instead, he or she will be encouraging the members of the group to discuss what they have learned. The leader will be asking the questions that are found in this guide.

3. Stick to the topic being discussed. Your answers should be based on the verses which are the focus of the discussion and not on outside authorities such as commentaries or speakers. These studies focus on a particular passage of Scripture. Only rarely should you refer to other portions of the Bible. This allows for everyone to participate in in-depth study on equal ground.

4. Be sensitive to the other members of the group. Listen attentively when they describe what they have learned. You may be surprised by their insights! Each question assumes a variety of answers. Many questions do not have "right" answers, particularly questions that aim at meaning or application. Instead the questions push us to explore the passage more thoroughly.

When possible, link what you say to the comments of others. Also, be affirming whenever you can. This will encourage some of the more hesitant members of the group to participate.

5. Be careful not to dominate the discussion. We are sometimes so eager to express our thoughts that we leave too little opportunity for others to respond. By all means participate! But allow others to also.

6. Expect God to teach you through the passage being discussed and through the other members of the group. Pray that you will have an enjoyable and profitable time together, but also that as a result of the study you will find ways that you can take action individually and/or as a group.

7. Remember that anything said in the group is considered confidential and should not be discussed outside the group unless specific permission is given to do so.

8. If you are the group leader, you will find additional suggestions at the back of the guide.

1

Strangers in the World

All of us have experienced times when we did not fit in: arriving over-dressed (or underdressed) for a social occasion, not knowing the language spoken around us, being in a setting as a minority race or gender, holding a single dissenting opinion in a hotly debated topic. But underneath these embarrassing and painful moments sometimes lurks a pervasive sense that maybe we don't fit anywhere—really.

GROUP DISCUSSION. Tell of a time when you felt out of place—like a stranger who did not belong.

PERSONAL REFLECTION. If you knew you were about to enter a difficult set of circumstances that would test your faith, how would you prepare yourself?

Early Christians were subject to many kinds of isolation. Though their faith originated in Judaism, the Jews rejected them because Christians saw Jesus as Messiah. Romans would eventually use Christians as scapegoats, blaming them for all sorts of political woes. And pagans saw Christians as atheists because they insisted on worshiping only one God. In this setting, Peter offers beleaguered first-century Christians (and us) a different kind of belonging. *Read 1 Peter 1:1-12.*

1. Imagine you are one of the early Christians receiving Peter's letter. After studying this opening section, what would motivate you to keep reading?

2. Study Peter's description of the people who were about to receive his letter (vv. 1-2). How does his description of them help explain why they were "strangers in the world"?

3. How does the introduction to Peter's letter help you appreciate the three persons of God?

4. Peter says that God has given his people "new birth." What does he say grows out of that new birth (vv. 3-5)?

5. Peter says in verse 6, "Now for a little while you may have had to suffer grief in all kinds of trials." If you were to hear that kind of message, what information in this paragraph might help you through the suffering (vv. 3-9)?

6. How does the future as Peter describes it here offer you hope in your own setting?

7. What did Peter believe to be true of genuine faith (vv. 7-9)?

8. Peter complimented his readers because they believed in Jesus and loved him—even though they had not seen him (v. 8). What questions do you think people today have to cope with because they have not personally seen Jesus?

9. When have you seen Jesus (through a person or event) in a way that increased your faith?

---

10. By what different routes did news of salvation come to the readers of Peter's letter (vv. 10-12)?

---

11. In what ways are Christians special—even when compared to Old Testament prophets and angels?

---

12. Peter refers to new birth, or salvation, throughout this passage as a central difference between Christians and the world. What tensions have you experienced because of this difference?

13. How does God's gift of salvation help you cope with these tensions?

Pray thanking God that you belong to him and that you have an eternal home with him and his people. If you have not yet come into God's family, ask (if you are able) that he continue to show you the way.

Now or Later

Review some of the people who came to mind as you considered question 9—people who have increased your faith. Write a letter of appreciation to one of them. If this is not possible, write a prayer of thanks to God for that person's influence in your life.

Suffering and joy are mixed in this section of Peter's letter—as they often are in our own lives. Consider the people and events that have brought you pain; consider also sources that have brought you joy. (Odd that they are sometimes the same sources.) In prayer, share all of this with your loving God, who understands the mixture far better than we do.

Read again 1 Peter 1:8-9. Meditate on love and joy as Peter describes them. Thank God for offering a joy that cannot be diminished by earthbound events. Then, as much as you are able, enjoy!

2

Called to Be Different

Being a Christian shapes us—sometimes in surprising ways. We discover God-given strengths and use them in ways we could not have imagined. But we also discover our flaws and learn the painful effort of overcoming those sins. God calls his people to be different: different from what they would be if they did not believe in Jesus and different from the unbelievers around them.

GROUP DISCUSSION. What surprising strengths (or weaknesses) have you discovered in yourself as part of your Christian growth?

PERSONAL REFLECTION. Think of a Christian (living or dead) you admire. In what ways has that person practiced holy living? Pray, thanking God for his or her influence in your life.

Peter opens this section of his letter with the admonition to "prepare your minds for action." *Read 1 Peter 1:13-25.*

1. What mental and physical actions should a follower of Christ pursue?

2. Peter lists several ways that followers of Jesus ought to respond to his gift of salvation. Define each of these responses more fully (vv. 13-16).

3. Select one of these responses. If you were to put that response on the front burner of your priorities, what changes would you have to make in your life?

4. Verse 15 says, "Be holy in all you do." How might an honest attempt to be holy by God's standards improve your relationships with people close to you?

In what situations might it make you, as verse 17 says, more like a stranger?

5. Why does Peter tell us that we ought to live in "reverent fear" (v. 17)?

6. What events from the past would help the recipients of Peter's letter to appreciate God's concern for them (vv. 18-21)?

7. How could the conditions that Peter describes in verses 21-25 promote sincere love among Christians?

8. In speaking of a Christian's relationships, Peter drew a contrast between "love for your brothers" and being "strangers in the world" (see vv. 1, 17 and 22). When have you felt sheltered by a family kind of love among believers?

9. What contrasts do you see in verses 21-25 between what is temporary and what is enduring?

10. Peter links the Word of God with salvation and new birth. (Compare verses 10, 12, 23 and 25.) What do you think Peter means when he says that this Word is "enduring" and "stands forever"?

11. The readers of Peter's letter learned of God's gift of salvation because it was preached to them. How have you learned about it?

12. If you were trying to convey to someone else the value of new birth in your life, what would you want that person to know?

Pray for one person you would like to introduce to Christ—and ask Jesus to present that opportunity to you.

Now or Later

Jesus gave his standard for holy living with a summary statement of the law: "Love the Lord your God with all your heart and with all your soul and with all your mind and with all your strength . . . [and] love your neighbor as yourself" (Mark 12:30-31). In prayerful silence ask God to reveal ways in which you fail to express love to him with your whole being. Next, ask that he bring to mind those people whom you do not favor as much as you favor yourself. Confess to God your specific failures to love in his holy way.

Jot a quick list of all you have to do today (or tomorrow). How could you begin to tackle this list with the goal "be holy in all you do" (1 Peter 1:15)?

3

Do I Want to Grow Up?

1 Peter 2:1-12

"Would you send me to school?" [Peter] inquired craftily.

"Yes."

"And then to an office?"

"I suppose so."

"Soon I should be a man?"

"Very soon."

"I don't want to go to school and learn solemn things," he told her passionately.

"I don't want to be a man. O Wendy's mother, if I was to wake up and feel there was a beard!"

"Peter," said Wendy the comforter, "I should love you in a beard." Mrs. Darling stretched out her arms to him, but he repulsed her.

"Keep back, lady, no one is going to catch me and make me a man."*

GROUP DISCUSSION. When have you wished, at least for a moment, that you were not an adult?

PERSONAL REFLECTION. What people and events has God used to move you toward maturity? Make a list or create a timeline. As

much as you are able, reenter those events, and thank God for what
happened then.

The apostle Peter opens this section of his letter by insisting that his
readers "grow up in your salvation." *Read 1 Peter 2:1-12.*

1. What characteristics of spiritual maturity do you find in this passage?

2. Peter speaks here of two aspects of Christian growth: individual
and corporate. How might the five inner sins of verse 1 damage our
relationships with other believers?

When have you seen this kind of damage?

3. What does the metaphor in verses 2-3 suggest about how we
should nurture spiritual growth?

4. How does belief or unbelief influence the way a person understands Jesus, the living Stone (vv. 4-8)?

What are some of the effects of these differing points of view?

5. What would you expect to see in a person who had imitated Jesus and become a "living stone"?

6. What reasons do the people here have to praise God (vv. 9-10)?

7. As you look more carefully at verse 9, think of Christians you know. What steps could you take in these Christian groups to live up to this description?

8. What inner and outer battles do you see in verses 11-12?

---

9. Verse 11 repeats a now familiar theme in 1 Peter—that Christians are aliens and strangers in the world. How might living up to the description of verse 9 cause a Christian to be alienated from the world?

---

10. The *New Bible Commentary* interprets verse 12, "the day [God] visits us," as "the day God will visit the earth and search out man's hearts in judgment."** If this were to occur in your lifetime, what evidence would you want God to find of your own spiritual growth?

---

11. How could today's passage help you overcome a tendency to be a spiritual Peter Pan?

Pray thanking God for specific forces he has brought into your life that have drawn you toward spiritual maturity. Ask for his care in further preparing you for the time when you will meet him face to face.

Now or Later

Take a prayerful look at spiritual maturity as Peter describes it in his letter. Place this alongside several areas of your life and evaluate your progress in that direction. Where appropriate, give yourself spiritual goals, noting a date when you will look back at your notes and evaluate your progress. The questions below may help guide your thinking and praying.

Malice, deceit, hypocrisy, envy and slander keep me from growing to spiritual maturity (v. 1). I need to root these out of my life by . . .

God calls me to spiritual maturity by joining me with other Christians as a "spiritual house" (v. 5), "a royal priesthood" and "a holy nation" (v. 9). I need to work on this spiritual connection with other Christians by . . .

Christian maturity means that I am never quite at home in this world. I am an alien and a stranger (v. 11) who wants to live in a way that causes even current non-Christians to "glorify God on the day he visits us" (v. 12). I will express my alien status in this world by . . .

*James M. Barrie, *Peter Pan* (New York: Charles Scribner's Sons, 1911), p. 228.
**D. Guthrie et al., eds., *The New Bible Commentary* (Grand Rapids, Mich.: Eerdmans, 1970), p. 124.

4

In His Steps

1 Peter 2:13—3:7

In the late 1800s, Charles Sheldon wrote a novel called *In His Steps* about a dying tramp who gets involved with the Rev. Henry Maxwell and his congregation. Through their experience with the tramp, this body of believers begins to see the submissive suffering of Jesus and what it means to walk "in his steps."

GROUP DISCUSSION. If you were to rate your natural inclination for being submissive on a scale of one to ten, where would you place yourself and why? (One is a mud-covered doormat; ten is a banner-waving firebrand.)

PERSONAL REFLECTION. As you try to follow the steps of Jesus, what do you value about that path?

What do you find difficult about walking in his steps?

Submission does not come easily to any of us, yet Peter thought it important—and he cites Jesus Christ as an example. *Read 1 Peter 2:13—3:7.*

1. Find several examples of submission in this passage. What is difficult about each?

_____

2. According to Peter, why should Christians treat their governing leaders with respect (2:13-15)?

_____

3. How could the teachings of 2:16-17 keep you from becoming a "muddy doormat" to your government?

_____

4. What connections does the text point out between Christ's suffering and a Christian's submission in the situation of slavery (2:18-21)?

_____

5. What were the effects of Christ's suffering (2:22-25)?

6. Verse 23 says that in his suffering Jesus "entrusted himself to him who judges justly." How might a similar trust in God help you to submit to the necessary suffering that has come into your own life?

7. Slowly and prayerfully reread the words of verse 24, substituting your own name for the appropriate pronouns. In what specific ways have you seen Christ's work here played out in your own experience?

8. In a society where wives rated barely above slaves, what can you find that is "progressive" about Peter's marriage principles in 3:1-7?

9. What reasons did Peter give for acting according to these principles?

10. Walking "in his steps" will often lead to submission—and even to suffering. In spite of this hardship, why might you choose this route?

11. What is one area in the foreseeable future where you could practice Christlike submission, and how would you do that?

Pray talking to God about the joy and the challenge of walking in the footprints of Jesus.

Finding a balance between responsible action for healthy change and submission to authority is a constant tension for the Christian who wants to obey this passage. How can you draw together both ends of this tension? (In what situations would you take action? At what point would you submit?) Consider what you should say and do

regarding civil government

in your job or school

in your marriage or in other relationships

5

If I'm Living Right, Then Why Do I Hurt So Much?

1 Peter 3:8-22

We often assume a direct connection between right living and easy living. It's an added pat on the back when life runs smoothly. But when suffering strikes, that assumption becomes an unspoken accusation. We turn on ourselves and question what we have done wrong, or (conversely) we feel that God has cheated us, as if he somehow owes us payment for our good behavior.

GROUP DISCUSSION. Bad things happen to good people—sometimes precisely because they are doing what is right and good. Why?

PERSONAL REFLECTION. When have you (or when has someone close to you) suffered because of doing what you believed to be right? Prayerfully review this situation, first examining your own motives and actions. Then in prayer, place the whole event into God's care and ask him to give you further understanding of it through this study.

Peter made no promises of easy living. Sometimes suffering comes—whether or not we earn it. It came to Jesus. *Read 1 Peter 3:8-22.*

1. What descriptions of right living and of suffering do you see in this passage?

2. Review verses 8-12. Find as many phrases as you can that describe what a Christian ought to be and do.

3. What reasons does Peter suggest for living that way?

4. What do you find difficult about the way of life described in verses 8-12?

What do you find attractive about that way of living?

5. Peter knew that in spite of godly living, Christians may encounter hardship. What counsel does Peter offer for coping with suffering (vv. 13-17)?

---

6. How could setting apart Christ as Lord, as verse 15 commands, help you endure suffering?

---

7. Why might unbelievers be willing to listen to reasons for hope from a person who is living the way Peter describes (vv. 15-17)?

---

8. Verse 18 is a capsule description of Christ's work and purpose. What can you know from this verse about why Jesus came and what he accomplished?

---

9. How was Christ's suffering similar to what Christians can expect?

10. Study the rather confusing information in verses 19-20. What is your best explanation of its meaning?

---

11. Why are Christians baptized (see vv. 21-22)?

---

12. Our world is often unjust. Bring to mind some of your past or current sufferings. In the context of these sufferings, how can the picture of Christ portrayed by this passage bring you hope?

Pray thanking God for Jesus who suffered for us, and for his presence with you in your own suffering.

Now or Later

Meditate on three sections of this passage:

1 Peter 3:8-9

1 Peter 3:10-12

1 Peter 3:18

Settle yourself into each passage at a time and place free of distractions. Focusing on one passage at a time, invite the work of God's Spirit to make these words from Peter's letter come alive in your being.

Ask God to point out significant phrases and to clarify their meaning in your mind.

Ask him to show you specific ways to bring your life into line with its teaching.

Use the text as a basis for prayer.

6

Christians at Risk

Persecution is part of life for Christians around the world. In China, Christian leaders are dangled from the ceiling with weights attached to their limbs to increase their pain. In Afghanistan, twelve Christian relief workers were on trial for their lives under the accusation of "proselytizing" among Muslim refugees. In Nigeria, Christian churches are burned to the ground at the hands of angry mobs.

GROUP DISCUSSION. If you were the object of the persecutions cited above, what do you hope that you would do? What questions would you be asking about God? What help would you want to receive from your Christian brothers and sisters? Make some notes together, which you will use at the end of the study.

PERSONAL REFLECTION. When you learn of Christians suffering because of their faith, what questions come to your mind? Make a list. (You will use it at the end of this study.)

When writing his letter, Peter assumed that "the end of all things is near" (4:7), and he knew that his Christian readers were at risk—at risk for falling away from the high standards of living that Jesus had set for his followers and at risk for deep and personal suffering because of their faith. *Read 1 Peter 4:1-11.*

1. Verse 1 draws attention to our attitude. What attitudes does this chapter ask Christians at risk to adopt?

---

2. According to Peter's opening paragraph, how is a Christian different from a pagan (vv. 1-6)? (Note actions as well as attitudes.)

---

3. The *New Bible Commentary* interprets verse 1 by saying that people who accept Christ's death for their own sins are symbolically linked to his suffering. In view of verse 2, what are some practical ways that Christians might live out that symbolic link with Jesus?

---

4. Our doubts sometimes taunt us. "Of what use is your Christian faith? God does not protect you. When your time comes, you die like the rest." How might the information in verses 4-6 help us deal with those doubts?

---

5. Notice Peter's beginning words in verse 7: "The end of all things is near." What emotional response do you think these words brought to his readers?

How do they make you feel? Why?

6. What specific instructions does Peter give suffering Christians who are aware that the end of all things is coming (vv. 7-11)?

7. Of what spiritual and practical value are these instructions?

8. Verse 11 speaks of two forms of leadership in the early church: those who speak (teach) and those who serve. How would the purpose of church leadership as it is described here prevent a misuse of power between Christians?

9. *Read 1 Peter 4:12-19.* According to these verses, what are some right and wrong ways for a Christian to suffer?

10. The term *Christian* is used only three times in the New Testament—here and in Acts 11:26 and 26:28. Used by outsiders, the word was probably a term of contempt, but to believers it meant "adopted into the family of Christ." Why might a Christian expect to sometimes encounter suffering because of that name?

11. How might verse 19 be both a comfort and a challenge to a Christian who suffers because of faith?

---

12. Look back to the questions you posed in the group discussion or personal reflection section. How do Peter's teachings help you deal with these questions?

Pray asking God to help you to "continue to do good" regardless of circumstances ahead.

Now or Later

Read the paper or watch the news looking for events that might bring suffering to Christians. Pray for your brothers and sisters there.

Consider writing to national or international authorities expressing your support for religious freedom and asking relief for Christians who are imprisoned or otherwise suffering for their faith. If you know names and locations of persecuted Christians, be as specific as you are able. Citizens of the United States may contact their national representatives through the Internet at <www.senate.gov> and <www.house.gov> or write to the president at

The White House
1600 Pennsylvania Ave.
Washington, DC 20500

International readers may write to

Secretary General
United Nations
United Nations Plaza
New York, NY 10017

7

TLC for
Trying Times

1 Peter 5

Relationships bring color to life. People add sparkle and fire to our existence. Some of this sparkle is the jagged red of controversy. Some is the orderly black and white of authority structure. And some is the comfortable amber of friendship.

GROUP DISCUSSION. Describe one of the more difficult relationships of your past. Then describe one of your most valuable relationships and what made it valuable.

PERSONAL REFLECTION. Take mental stock of your current relationships. What is one of your most difficult relationships at this point? What makes it difficult? What current relationship do you value most? Why? In prayer, invite God into these relationships, asking his help where you need it and giving him thanks for those relationships that you value most.

When Peter concluded his first letter, a work frequently pointing to suffering, he did not tell his readers to escape to the isolation of a spiritual or literal mountaintop. Instead, he pointed to their relationships and said, "Here's how to take care of each other." *Read 1 Peter 5.*

---

1. What various relationships do you see in this chapter?

---

2. Peter speaks in verse 1 to his fellow elders. In what ways did Peter see himself as like the elders he was writing to (vv. 1-4)?

---

3. If you were to use verses 1-4 to write a personality profile for a church elder, what would you include?

---

4. What would you put in an elder's job description?

---

5. When have you appreciated a person who acted toward you as a spiritual elder?

6. What different beings or groups must Christians ordinarily respond to (vv. 5-11)?

7. What instructions does Peter give in verses 5-9?

8. What reasons did Peter give for following each of these commands?

9. God's Word speaks to us in a variety of ways. What joy, comfort or warning in Peter's instructions (vv. 5-11) stands out to you?

10. In this chapter, Peter points out three forces on our lives: other Christians, Satan and God himself. How would you summarize an appropriate response to each?

11. Find as many phrases as you can that describe Peter's own relationships and his instructions for relationships among his readers (vv. 12-14).

---

12. Even in this last chapter of his letter, Peter three times mentions the theme of suffering. But in spite of the possibility of suffering, Peter instructs his readers in verse 12 to "stand fast" in the grace of God. How could Peter's teachings about relationships in this chapter help you to "stand fast" in your own faith?

Pray thanking God for the relationship he offers you with himself.

Now or Later

Review your relationships as you outlined them in group discussion or personal reflection. What do you find in this chapter that might bring spiritual health to one of your more difficult relationships?

Pray that God will make the necessary changes in you, then take at least one step toward healing that relationship.

Reread this chapter, looking for one or more sentences that might be God's word for you. Receive them into yourself with thanksgiving. Express your appreciation or your resolutions to your loving God.

Read verses 10-11 as a prayer of blessing, inserting the name of a person you are praying for.

8

The Long
Way Home

What is the way to heaven? Is it by proper knowledge of Christian doctrines? Or by godly living? Is it by faith in Christ's gift of salvation? Or by working according to Christ's goals and principles? Is it by God's call to us to be his own? Or by our own endurance with God until the day we die? Weighty issues. And with them, Peter opens his second letter.

GROUP DISCUSSION. Scripture doesn't give us much specific information about heaven, perhaps to allow us creativity as we look forward to that time. What are some of your favorite imaginations of heaven?

PERSONAL REFLECTION. We sometimes hear the apology, "Be patient with me. God isn't finished with me yet." What do you think God is working to accomplish in you as he prepares you for eternity with him?

After writing an earlier letter telling his readers to expect suffering as a part of this life, Peter now writes a second letter. This time he points toward the end of life: our eternal reward—whether it comes at our death or at Christ's return. *Read 2 Peter 1:1-11.*

1. Peter opens his second letter by saying that God "has given us everything we need for life and godliness" (v. 3). What does godliness look like according to these verses?

2. What do verses 1-2 tell us about the writer and readers of this letter—and the relationship between them?

3. In verses 1-2 we are told that we will receive the gifts of faith, grace and peace through Christ's righteousness and knowledge of God. How does your own spiritual well-being depend in part on Christ's righteousness and in part on your knowledge of God?

4. Verse 3 is sometimes called the key to Peter's second letter. What all would you expect to find in a book with this verse as an introduction?

5. Verse 3 speaks of both knowledge and holy living as a part of the Christian life. Think of the balance between knowledge of Jesus and holy living that you have seen in Christians. What happens if one area or the other is weak?

6. What do Christ's power and promises give to those who accept him (vv. 1-4)?

7. Peter writes in verse 4 that because of God's promises, Christians "may participate in the divine nature and escape the corruption in the world." What does he then expect believers to do to nurture their own holy living (vv. 5-7)?

8. How are knowledge of Jesus and godly living related to each other (vv. 8-9)?

9. Select one of the Christian qualities mentioned in verses 5-7 that you would like to have become more prominent in your own life. If you were to practice this quality more faithfully, how would it help you escape the pollution of evil influences around you?

How would it complement your knowledge of Jesus Christ?

10. What do you think it means for a person to be called and elected by God (vv. 10-11)?

11. What is the normal effect of this call and election on a person's life—and future?

12. Verse 3 says that the divine power of Jesus has given us everything we need for godliness here and also for eternal life. If you were to draw more fully on this power that Jesus makes available to you, what changes would you hope to see in yourself?

As much as you are able, picture yourself in "the eternal kingdom of our Lord and Savior Jesus Christ" (v. 11). Thank God for that future that he is preparing for you even now. Ask that he will also prepare you for that time.

Now or Later

Verse 3 says that God has given us "everything we need" to take us on the long route to our eternal home with him. Take time to enumerate some of those needs that God has met:

Consider Jesus' sacrifice for you.

Remember how you first came to know of Christ's love.

Recognize the magnetic power of the Holy Spirit as he drew you to faith.

Think of how God has developed your character through both the painful and joyful events of your life.

Create a page or so of journal notes that reflect what God's gift of granting "everything we need" has been in your life. Then thank God for this work that he is doing in you.

9

If I Should Die . . .

Joe Bayley was a devout Christian who influenced many for Christ through his writing (especially a book titled *Heaven*) and, more important, through his life. Ten years after writing *Heaven*, he lay on a gurney outside an operating room, waiting to undergo heart surgery. At Mayo's famed Methodist Hospital, this surgery was routine. Joe expected to be walking around the hospital hallways in a few days. But he wasn't. Instead, hours later, Joe walked into eternity.

GROUP DISCUSSION. If you thought you might be conveying a final message to people you hoped would continue in their Christian faith, who would you speak or write to? What would you want them to know? Where would you refer them for continued support of their faith?

PERSONAL REFLECTION. Who has been a spiritual rock for you, a person (perhaps a biblical writer) who helped you believe and keep on believing? Offer your thanks to God for that person.

Peter's second letter was one of his final works. Peter knew that this letter might be his last words to those who read it. So he reminded them of the source of their faith and directed them to a variety of reference points that could help them to keep on believing. *Read 2 Peter 1:12-21.*

1. Peter says, "I think it is right to refresh your memory" (v. 13). What people and events does he remind them of (vv. 16-21)?

---

2. What responsibilities did Peter seem to feel he had for his readers (vv. 12-15)?

---

3. What phrases here create a picture of Peter's view of death?

Based on these phrases, how would you describe Peter's attitude about death?

---

4. What do you hope will be your own feelings when you approach death?

5. What could you be doing during your lifetime to build toward a "good death"?

---

6. In verses 16-18 Peter refers to Christ's transfiguration. Read Matthew 17:1-8. In what different ways did this event show Christ's majesty?

---

7. What difference would it make to those who knew Peter that his teachings about Jesus came from "eyewitnesses of his majesty"?

---

8. What difference does it make to you that God said of Jesus, "This is my Son, whom I love; with him I am well pleased. Listen to him!" (Matthew 17:5).

---

9. What does 2 Peter 1:19-21 show about the origin and purpose of Scripture?

10. What are some ways that you can show an appropriate respect for Scripture?

---

11. Peter did not want his readers to be so dependent on him that their faith would fall apart after his death. (Perhaps he knew that some new believers depend too much on other Christians.) So here Peter pointed to the only basis for real faith: Jesus Christ as he is revealed in Scripture. Who would you like to influence with your faith in your lifetime, and how can you best go about it?

Pray for those who came to your mind as you reflected on the question above. Ask God to create opportunities that will lead to shared faith. Then prepare yourself to do so.

Now or Later

Peter says that his readers should pay attention to the prophets "as a light shining in a dark place, until the day dawns" (v. 19). Read and meditate on several prophets who spoke of Christ. Thank God for what you find there.

Isaiah 40:1-11

Isaiah 53:1-12

Micah 5:2-5

Zechariah 9:9

Revelation 21:22—22:7

10

Follow
Which Leader?

Is anything true—really? Is Christianity whatever you want it to be, or are there realities in the Christian faith that make anything less than those truths non-Christian? In an age where many people think that a good religion is any belief that brings you comfort, the apostle Peter's voice sounds a strident objection: Some beliefs are true Christianity. And some beliefs are false—and therefore not Christian at all. He challenges his readers to learn the difference.

GROUP DISCUSSION. Some religions are almost Christian—but not quite. When and how have you come in contact with one of these belief systems? What concerns did this encounter raise in your mind?

PERSONAL REFLECTION. Consider sources you use to shape your concept of what is truly Christian: Scripture? ancient confessions, creeds and catechisms? religious books? spiritual leaders? Evaluate the reliability of these sources, how you choose them, on what basis you interpret Scripture and what cautions you have in place to protect yourself from falling into a form of Christianity that is less than genuine. Pray about your observations.

As Peter continues preparing his readers to hang onto their faith without him, he addresses the dangers of heresy and "false teachers" who tempt Christians their direction. *Read 2 Peter 2.*

---

1. This chapter is like a danger signal along a treacherous road leading to heresy. What warnings do you find here? (Look back at 1:20-21 as well.)

---

2. Why are false teachers dangerous (1:20—2:3)?

---

3. Study verses 4-9. What did Peter want his readers to learn from these Old Testament events?

---

4. How can knowledge of these Old Testament events help you endure environments around you that oppose true teachings about God?

---

5. What characteristics should alert us that we are encountering a false teacher (vv. 10-19)?

---

6. Why might some people be attracted to teachers with these charac-teristics?

---

7. Verse 19 says that false teachers may promise freedom. What kinds of freedom might a new or weak Christian find enticing?

---

8. How might these "freedoms" become another form of slavery?

---

9. Compare Christ's work in 2 Peter 1:1-4 with the freedom and sla-very of verse 19. How is the gift Christ offers different from the offer-ing of a false teacher?

10. Why might it be better if a false teacher had never known the truth (vv. 20-22)?

---

11. How can you protect yourself from the influence of false teachers?

---

12. What cautions can you institute to keep from becoming a false teacher yourself?

Pray for someone you know who is leaning toward a faith that is less than Christian.

Now or Later

In the year 325 some three hundred Christian bishops gathered from the far reaches of the then-known world and met at a town named Nicea in what is now northwest Turkey. Some of these Christians still bore wounds of persecution for their faith. Their purpose was to create a clear, concise statement of the Christian faith. After several months of careful study of Scripture they created the Nicene Creed, a basic statement still held as foundational Christian truth by Protestants and Catholics alike. Most heresies, when placed beside the Nicene Creed, reveal themselves to be less than Christian.

In the days ahead, spend time meditating on each line of this document, letting its full meaning sink into your soul. In prayer, praise God for himself as he is reveled in the faith of these ancient Christians.

We believe in God, the Father Almighty,
  Maker of heaven and earth,
  of all things visible and invisible.

And in one Lord Jesus Christ, the only-begotten Son of God,
  begotten of his Father before all worlds,
  God of God, Light of Light,
  very God of very God,
  begotten, not made, being of one substance with the Father;
  by whom all things were made;
  who for us and for our salvation
  came down from heaven,
  and was incarnate by the Holy Spirit of the virgin Mary,
  and was made man;
  and was crucified also for us under Pontius Pilate;
  he suffered and was buried;
  and the third day he rose again according to the Scriptures,
  and ascended into heaven, and is seated at the right hand of the Father;
  and he shall come again, with glory, to judge both the living
    and the dead;
  whose kingdom shall have no end.

And we believe in the Holy Spirit, the Lord and giver of life,
  who proceeds from the Father and the Son;
  who with the Father and the Son together is worshiped and glorified;
  who spoke by the prophets;
  and we believe in one holy catholic and apostolic church;
  we acknowledge one baptism for the remission of sins;
  and we look for the resurrection of the dead,
  and the life of the world to come. Amen.

—*Council of Nicea, 325*

11

The Fire
Next Time

This world will end sometime, somehow, as Scripture has promised. At times that promise seems like a threat, a cruel interruption to a life full of hope not yet fulfilled. But at other times, when troubles loom and solutions defy our best efforts, that promise of an end feels like welcome relief.

GROUP DISCUSSION. If you were to paint a painting (or compose a piece of music) titled "The End of the World," what would you put in it?

PERSONAL REFLECTION. When are you most likely to wish the world would end? Why? Take these feelings and circumstances to God in prayer, asking his relief. Ask for healing hope, not only for the world to come but also for the life that he gives you in this world.

The final chapter of Peter's final letter speaks of an end, but an end with hope. *Read 2 Peter 3.*

1. If you were one of the early readers of this letter, what ideas in this chapter would cause you to pay attention?

2. Verse 4 says that scoffers will ask, "Where is this 'coming' he promised?" Read two of those promises in John 14:1-3 and Acts 1:6-11. If you were living thirty or forty years after Christ's death and resurrection, what questions would you be asking about his return?

3. What questions do you ask now?

4. What mistakes will the last-day scoffers make (vv. 4-11)?

5. What reasons does Peter offer for a delay in Christ's return?

6. What words and phrases throughout this passage help describe the day of the Lord?

---

7. Compare and contrast the use of fire and water in this passage. What is the significance of each?

---

8. Notice the question of verse 11, "What kind of people ought you to be?" What answers can you find throughout the remainder of the chapter?

---

9. Why might living this way prepare you for the kind of day described here?

---

10. Over and over in this passage, we see words of destruction. In view of this, why do you think Peter says three times that we are to "look forward to" this day and even speed its coming?

11. If the day of the Lord were to come in your lifetime, what would you like to accomplish first?

In what condition would you like God to find your work?

your relationships?

your status with him?

Pray thanking God that he is in charge of all things, that nothing (even the end of the world) is beyond his control. Invite God to prepare you for meeting him—however and whenever that occurs.

Now or Later

Read Revelation 22, the last chapter of the New Testament. Picture yourself in this scene, and thank God for what you find there.

The last prayer of the New Testament invites Jesus' return with the words, "Come, Lord Jesus" (Revelation 22:20). If you are able to do so honestly, pray this prayer as your own.

12

The Twisted Fate of Twisted Faith

Jude

In November 1978, in a jungle clearing of Guyana, more than nine hundred people committed suicide by drinking cyanide-treated punch. Those too young to act on their own were given the punch by their parents. The Jonestown massacre sends a shudder through all Christians—and well it should—because Jim Jones, who prescribed this "White Night" of death, at one time claimed to be one of our own.

GROUP DISCUSSION. How do you think people get tricked into perverted versions of the Christian faith?

PERSONAL REFLECTION. What do you value about the Christian faith? Thank God for the place he has given you within this body of authentic believers.

Jude's book is similar to 2 Peter 2. It warns us of false teachings and false faiths. *Read the book of Jude.*

1. What descriptions do you see here of people who hold a false kind of religion?

2. What do the first two verses tell you about the writer of this letter and the people he wrote to?

3. What can you know of the circumstances of the people receiving this letter and of Jude's purpose in writing to them (vv. 3-4)?

4. Find as many words and phrases as you can in this letter that describe those "certain men" who have "secretly slipped in among you."

5. What harm could people like these do within a body of believers?

6. Why might it be hard to resist their influence?

7. Notice that one of the problems of these false teachers was that they denied "Jesus Christ our only Sovereign and Lord" (v. 4). Study each word of that name for Jesus. How can the beliefs behind each of those words keep a Christian from straying into theological error?

---

8. Note eight references to characters of Jewish history and literature in verses 5-11. What appears to be Jude's purpose in pointing out these characters and events?

---

9. Jude uses a series of six metaphors in verses 12-13. How does each illustrate the danger of teachers who have perverted the gospel?

---

10. In the face of this problem, Jude gives his readers two sets of instructions: "remember" (v. 17) and "build yourselves up" (v. 20). Notice the specific instructions under each of these. How would remembering in the way Jude describes help believers keep the essential ingredients of the Christian faith?

How would building ourselves up in the ways Jude outlines (vv. 20-23) help us keep on living in a way that is true to our faith?

11. The doxology of verses 24-25 frequently closes Christian services of worship. Notice its description of God's power and his character. How might a group of Christians troubled by infiltrated false teachings of life and doctrine take courage from these words?

12. What errors in faith and life do you see as subtle dangers to today's Christians?

13. How can you protect yourself, and other believers whose lives you touch, from falling into these errors?

Pray, asking God's protection on your faith.

Now or Later

Pray or sing Jude's doxology of verses 24-25 as your own praise to God.

Pray or sing it again, enjoying its blessing of God's protection as if this doxology were being prayed over you.

Pray the content of this blessing for various people, inserting their names as you pray God's keeping power on them.

Leader's Notes

Leading a Bible discussion can be an enjoyable and rewarding experience. But it can also be *scary*—especially if you've never done it before. If this is your feeling, you're in good company. When God asked Moses to lead the Israelites out of Egypt, he replied, "O Lord, please send someone else to do it"! (Ex 4:13). It was the same with Solomon, Jeremiah and Timothy, but God helped these people in spite of their weaknesses, and he will help you as well.

You don't need to be an expert on the Bible or a trained teacher to lead a Bible discussion. The idea behind these inductive studies is that the leader guides group members to discover for themselves what the Bible has to say. This method of learning will allow group members to remember much more of what is said than a lecture would.

These studies are designed to be led easily. As a matter of fact, the flow of questions through the passage from observation to interpretation to application is so natural that you may feel that the studies lead themselves. This study guide is also flexible. You can use it with a variety of groups—student, professional, neighborhood or church groups. Each study takes forty-five to sixty minutes in a group setting.

There are some important facts to know about group dynamics and encouraging discussion. The suggestions listed below should enable you to effectively and enjoyably fulfill your role as leader.

Preparing for the Study

1. Ask God to help you understand and apply the passage in your own life. Unless this happens, you will not be prepared to lead others. Pray too for the various members of the group. Ask God to open your hearts to the message of his Word and motivate you to action.

2. Read the introduction to the entire guide to get an overview of the

entire book and the issues which will be explored.

3. As you begin each study, read and reread the assigned Bible passage to familiarize yourself with it.

4. This study guide is based on the New International Version of the Bible. It will help you and the group if you use this translation as the basis for your study and discussion.

5. Carefully work through each question in the study. Spend time in meditation and reflection as you consider how to respond.

6. Write your thoughts and responses in the space provided in the study guide. This will help you to express your understanding of the passage clearly.

7. It might help to have a Bible dictionary handy. Use it to look up any unfamiliar words, names or places. (For additional help on how to study a passage, see chapter five of *How to Lead a LifeGuide Bible Study*, InterVarsity Press.)

8. Consider how you can apply the Scripture to your life. Remember that the group will follow your lead in responding to the studies. They will not go any deeper than you do.

9. Once you have finished your own study of the passage, familiarize yourself with the leader's notes for the study you are leading. These are designed to help you in several ways. First, they tell you the purpose the study guide author had in mind when writing the study. Take time to think through how the study questions work together to accomplish that purpose. Second, the notes provide you with additional background information or suggestions on group dynamics for various questions. This information can be useful when people have difficulty understanding or answering a question. Third, the leader's notes can alert you to potential problems you may encounter during the study.

10. If you wish to remind yourself of anything mentioned in the leader's notes, make a note to yourself below that question in the study.

Leading the Study

1. Begin the study on time. Open with prayer, asking God to help the group to understand and apply the passage.

2. Be sure that everyone in your group has a study guide. Encourage the group to prepare beforehand for each discussion by reading the introduction to the guide and by working through the questions in the study.

3. At the beginning of your first time together, explain that these studies are meant to be discussions, not lectures. Encourage the members of the group to participate. However, do not put pressure on those who may be hes-

itant to speak during the first few sessions. You may want to suggest the following guidelines to your group.

☐ Stick to the topic being discussed.

☐ Your responses should be based on the verses which are the focus of the discussion and not on outside authorities such as commentaries or speakers.

☐ These studies focus on a particular passage of Scripture. Only rarely should you refer to other portions of the Bible. This allows for everyone to participate in in-depth study on equal ground.

☐ Anything said in the group is considered confidential and will not be discussed outside the group unless specific permission is given to do so.

☐ We will listen attentively to each other and provide time for each person present to talk.

☐ We will pray for each other.

4. Have a group member read the introduction at the beginning of the discussion.

5. Every session begins with a group discussion question. The question or activity is meant to be used before the passage is read. The question introduces the theme of the study and encourages group members to begin to open up. Encourage as many members as possible to participate, and be ready to get the discussion going with your own response.

This section is designed to reveal where our thoughts or feelings need to be transformed by Scripture. That is why it is especially important not to read the passage before the discussion question is asked. The passage will tend to color the honest reactions people would otherwise give because they are, of course, supposed to think the way the Bible does.

You may want to supplement the group discussion question with an icebreaker to help people to get comfortable. See the community section of *Small Group Idea Book* for more ideas.

You also might want to use the personal reflection question with your group. Either allow a time of silence for people to respond individually or discuss it together.

6. Have a group member (or members if the passage is long) read aloud the passage to be studied. Then give people several minutes to read the passage again silently so that they can take it all in.

7. Question 1 will generally be an overview question designed to briefly survey the passage. Encourage the group to look at the whole passage, but try to avoid getting sidetracked by questions or issues that will be addressed later in the study.

8. As you ask the questions, keep in mind that they are designed to be

used just as they are written. You may simply read them aloud. Or you may prefer to express them in your own words.

There may be times when it is appropriate to deviate from the study guide. For example, a question may have already been answered. If so, move on to the next question. Or someone may raise an important question not covered in the guide. Take time to discuss it, but try to keep the group from going off on tangents.

9. Avoid answering your own questions. If necessary, repeat or rephrase them until they are clearly understood. Or point out something you read in the leader's notes to clarify the context or meaning. An eager group quickly becomes passive and silent if they think the leader will do most of the talking.

10. Don't be afraid of silence. People may need time to think about the question before formulating their answers.

11. Don't be content with just one answer. Ask, "What do the rest of you think?" or "Anything else?" until several people have given answers to the question.

12. Acknowledge all contributions. Try to be affirming whenever possible. Never reject an answer. If it is clearly off-base, ask, "Which verse led you to that conclusion?" or again, "What do the rest of you think?"

13. Don't expect every answer to be addressed to you, even though this will probably happen at first. As group members become more at ease, they will begin to truly interact with each other. This is one sign of healthy discussion.

14. Don't be afraid of controversy. It can be very stimulating. If you don't resolve an issue completely, don't be frustrated. Move on and keep it in mind for later. A subsequent study may solve the problem.

15. Periodically summarize what the group has said about the passage. This helps to draw together the various ideas mentioned and gives continuity to the study. But don't preach.

16. At the end of the Bible discussion you may want to allow group members a time of quiet to work on an idea under "Now or Later." Then discuss what you experienced. Or you may want to encourage group members to work on these ideas between meetings. Give an opportunity during the session for people to talk about what they are learning.

17. Conclude your time together with conversational prayer, adapting the prayer suggestion at the end of the study to your group. Ask for God's help in following through on the commitments you've made.

18. End on time.

Many more suggestions and helps are found in *How to Lead a LifeGuide Bible Study*, which is part of the LifeGuide Bible Study series.

Components of Small Groups

A healthy small group should do more than study the Bible. There are four components to consider as you structure your time together.

Nurture. Small groups help us to grow in our knowledge and love of God. Bible study is the key to making this happen and is the foundation of your small group.

Community. Small groups are a great place to develop deep friendships with other Christians. Allow time for informal interaction before and after each study. Plan activities and games that will help you get to know each other. Spend time having fun together—going on a picnic or cooking dinner together.

Worship and prayer. Your study will be enhanced by spending time praising God together in prayer or song. Pray for each other's needs—and keep track of how God is answering prayer in your group. Ask God to help you to apply what you are learning in your study.

Outreach. Reaching out to others can be a practical way of applying what you are learning, and it will keep your group from becoming self-focused. Host a series of evangelistic discussions for your friends or neighbors. Clean up the yard of an elderly friend. Serve at a soup kitchen together, or spend a day working on a Habitat house.

Many more suggestions and helps in each of these areas are found in *Small Group Idea Book*. Information on building a small group can be found in *Small Group Leaders' Handbook* and *The Big Book on Small Groups* (both from Inter-Varsity Press). Reading through one of these books would be worth your time.

Study 1. 1 Peter 1:1-12. Strangers in the World.

Purpose: To appreciate God's gift of salvation.

Group discussion. Be prepared to open with a rather lighthearted story from your own experiences—just in case people need a few moments to gather their own memories. But as the storytelling commences, invite those who wish to tell of more painful settings to share. A major theme in Peter's letter is suffering, in part because Christians are really not at home in this world. In the eternal sense, we do not *belong* here. So a sense of alienation and suffering is to be expected.

Question 1. Use this overview question first to put yourselves in the position of its original readers and second to survey the general tone and details of information that Peter uses to lead his readers into the body of his letter.

Question 2. Use this question to examine more closely verses 1 and 2. Note that the readers of Peter's letter were "God's elect," and thereby separate from the world at large; that they were "scattered"; that they were "chosen," possibly creating a sense of elitism from outsiders; that they were chosen through the "sanctifying" (setting apart) work of the Spirit; that they practiced "obedience" to Jesus Christ. All of this together would create a "stranger" relationship with the world.

Question 4. If you were to diagram the sentence beginning with verse 3, you would find that virtually all of the information in verses 3-5 hinges on "new birth." Pick out all this information, but don't stop with a mere recitation of the facts. Continue by considering how these various aspects of new birth relate to each other.

Question 5. Draw answers from throughout verses 3-9.

Question 6. If you are leading a group, help people to respond to this question by moving from the more general discussion of hope in the midst of suffering to specific effects on their own current situation.

Question 7. Almost all that Peter says in verses 7-9 helps define what he means by genuine faith—and its results. Use this question to carefully analyze these verses.

Question 8. If you are in a group, first try to get at least one question from each person. Then let those who have several questions continue to add to the list until you feel that you have covered the topic.

Question 12. Answers to this question provide a backdrop for the final question, so be thorough.

Question 13. If answers are slow in coming, look at the various aspects of salvation revealed in 1 Peter 1:1-12, and then consider how salvation touches our own setting.

Study 2. 1 Peter 1:13-25. Called to Be Different.

Purpose: To respond to God's gift of salvation with holy imitation of Jesus.

Question 2. Help your group spot the five commands in verses 13-16. To define each fully might take hours, so settle for a fairly concise general definition of each.

Question 4. Discuss the first question briefly in order to set up a contrasting framework for the second question.

Question 6. Your group should examine the following past events noted throughout the passage: "You were redeemed" (v. 18); "the empty way of life [was] handed down to you" (v. 18); "he was chosen before the creation of the world" (v. 20); he "was revealed" (v. 20); "you believe" (v. 21); "God . . . raised him from the dead and glorified him" (v. 21). Each of these events from the past had a bearing on the current condition of those who received Peter's letter.

Question 7. Discuss first the conditions outlined in verses 21 and 22. Then, if time permits, add other conditions revealed thus far in Peter's letter.

Question 9. A chart may help understand this contrast. Items would include the following:

Temporary	Enduring
all people (v. 24)	new birth (v. 23)
flowers (v. 24)	Word of God (vv. 23, 25)
grass (v. 24)	
glory of men (v. 24)	

Question 10. Compare verses 10, 12 (from the previous study), 23 and 25 so that you can better understand the flow of Peter's reasoning. These verses trace God's redeeming work from the age of the prophets who searched for information about Christ's coming—but did not themselves experience it. They "served" the believers of Peter's era with their preparation. It was part of the "imperishable seed" presented to the new Christian church—the "word" that Peter preached. Help your group to thoughtfully expand on these themes.

Study 3. 1 Peter 2:1-12. Do I Want to Grow Up?

Purpose: To desire spiritual growth.

Group Discussion. People in your group may remember funny examples of this kind, or more serious ones. An adult Peter Pan is only a shadowy shape of an adult. Yet many of us have wanted to turn cartwheels in spring grass— and maybe done so! Potential follow-up questions include: In what ways would it be tempting to follow Peter Pan's approach to life? What happens when a person refuses to grow up? Why might some Christians intentionally limit their spiritual growth?

Question 1. This question should lead to an overview of the passage. Notice characteristics inhibiting spiritual maturity in verse 1. Also note that our maturity begins with God; he chooses us (v. 4). The implications of being chosen by God become more fully evident in our relationships with other believers, as described in verses 9-10, and are lived out in particular ways that point to an eternal future (vv. 11-12). If you need a clarifying question, try, "What forces do you see in this passage that lead a person toward spiritual maturity?"

Question 2. Don't settle for a mere recitation of the sins listed in verse 1. Discuss how each one corrupts Christian relationships. Most churches and families provide ready examples.

Question 3. The verbs contained in these verses will help your group think of appropriate actions. People should spot such phrases as "rid yourselves," "taste" (compared with "crave") and "grow up." They may also notice the natural process these verbs convey—as if growing is the normal thing to do.

Question 4. Ask your group to begin discussion of these questions with phrases from the passage. (The group should find several phrases that represent the two opposing points of view.) Once people have taken appropriate note of these, they can begin to discuss the differing effects of belief and unbelief.

Verse 8 may raise the question "Does God destine some people to be eternally lost?" *The New Bible Commentary* hedges with this answer: "Destined need not imply more than that those who disobey the Word of God, both written and living, are bound to find that instead of being the foundation on which to build, he is embarrassingly in their way and will sooner or later cause them to trip and fall" (D. Guthrie, J. A. Motyer, A. M. Stibbs, D. J. Wiseman, eds., *The New Bible Commentary* [Grand Rapids, Mich.: Eerdmans, 1970], p. 1241).

Question 5. As your group attempts to describe the kind of people these verses reflect, it will discover a corporate relationship. Key phrases include "spiritual house," "holy priesthood," "sacrifices" (a giving nature), "acceptable" (implies obedience to God), "precious" (speaks of an attitude of worship). As the discussion of this question progresses, the group should flesh out these terms—and others from verses 4-8—with current-day actions and personalities. If you need a follow-up question, ask, "What do you want to see in other Christians?"

Question 6. What is the "royal priesthood"? *The New Bible Commentary* points out that throughout Old Testament history a division existed between kingly functions and priestly functions. In fact, King Saul received severe condemnation from Samuel when he attempted to combine the two roles (see 1 Sam 13:5-15). But believers in Christ are both royalty and priests before God.

Question 8. Consider both what we *are* together as well as what we *do*.

Study 4. 1 Peter 2:13—3:7. In His Steps.

Purpose: To follow Christ's example of submission and to hold this in tension with responsible action for change.

Question 1. Submission to government, masters and spouses are obvious answers. Notice also that Jesus submitted to those who caused his suffering. These four points form an outline for the rest of the study.

Question 2. Find four or five reasons in the text.

Question 4. The Greek word translated here as "slave" also includes hired servants.

Question 5. Note several similarities between the suffering of a slave in verses 18-20 and the sufferings of Jesus in verses 21-25.

Question 7. Allow a few moments of silence for people to read and pray through the text and then follow-up with the question.

Question 8. Wifely submission hardly sounds progressive in today's society. Indeed, it is likely to raise the neck hairs of almost any contemporary woman—married or single. A few observations from the text may put this into perspective.

Your group should note the words "in the same way" of verse 1. This probably refers to the actions of Christ himself in 2:23—"he entrusted himself to him [the father] who judges justly." Jesus is God, yet by taking human form, therefore subject to suffering, he entrusted himself to his Father. In much the same way, a woman today entrusts herself to her husband in her marriage vows. She submits some of her rights and freedoms to her husband's care.

Paul's command of wifely submission does not permit emotional or physical abuse. Paul's instructions to husbands (3:7) prohibit that kind of relationship. Paul commands husbands to "respect" their wives, to treat them as "heirs with you of [God's] gracious gift of life." In Christian marriages submission and respect must walk hand in hand. A husband who respects his wife does not make her a doormat. And a wife who commands respect will not allow it.

Study 5. 1 Peter 3:8-22. If I'm Living Right, Then Why Do I Hurt So Much?

Purpose: To find hope, in spite of suffering, because of Jesus.

Group discussion. Many long books have been written in an attempt to answer this question, yet people continue to struggle with it, particularly when suffering comes to them. Consider first going around the circle of your group and asking each person to give his or her best two-sentence answer to the question. Then discuss the implications of what you have said. Topics should include a variety of subjects, for example, the meaning of the term *good*. (Are any of us good—when compared to God's standards for righteousness?) You will probably also touch on the nature of God, the purposes of suffering, the nature of a world that is polluted by human sin, God's power and his love—as well as his providence. If you want to approach this subject with a personal rather than theological pattern, ask, When have you seen bad things happen to a person who was only trying to do what was right and good? What do you hope would be your response if it happened to you?

Question 1. Use this question to survey the passage, looking for mentions of right living and also of suffering. Don't pause too long to examine connections between the two at this point. Later questions will help you form these links.

Question 2. Find about ten appropriate phrases.

Question 3. Answers appear in verses 9-12.

Question 9. See especially verse 18. The opening phrase "for Christ" serves as a pivot point in the passage. When we suffer because of doing good, we do not do so alone. Christ did the same—and for out benefit. Compare Christ's work as it is described here with the way of living that Peter advocates for believers. "The righteous for the unrighteous" says that Christ's suffering was not deserved. "To bring you to God" speaks of a selflessness about his suffering. It was other-centered.

Question 10. The Apostles' Creed includes as a descriptive phrase about Jesus: "He descended into hell." That phrase comes from this biblical text along with several others. Verses 19-20 raise the question, Where did Jesus go and who did he speak to when he "preached to the spirits in prison?" Bible scholars pose many possible interpretations. One possibility is that Jesus preached to those who died prior to his coming to earth, thus giving them an opportunity to hear, repent and believe. A second view is that Jesus preached to the fallen angels who had joined Satan's side. He announced his victory over them—and his triumph over death. You may see other possible explanations; just be sure that they fit with the information in the text and its context.

Question 11. Christians hold a variety of views on baptism. If you are meeting with a group, be sure to treat with respect the baptismal beliefs of other Christians present. Be aware also that in order to form a complete theology of baptism, you would need to integrate all biblical references on the subject. For the purpose of understanding this particular passage, be sure to use all of the information in verses 21 and 22, using the question to examine the symbolism and meaning of baptism as Peter presents it here. For example, you will need to consider how the flood of Noah's era symbolizes Christian baptism. The flood and Christ's death both emphasized God's judgment on sin. But they each also brought new life. The rite of baptism unites these two themes of judgment and deliverance.

Question 12. Qualities of Jesus that might help make some sense of suffering appear in verses 15, 18 and 21-22. Use this question to encourage each other to hope—because of Jesus.

If you want a more personal follow-up question ask, "What is one choice you made in the last few months that you anticipated would bring some form of suffering? What happened? What did you learn from the experience?"

Study 6. 1 Peter 4. Christians at Risk.

Purpose: To prepare Christians to endure suffering for their faith.

Group discussion and personal reflection. Explore questions about God, the world or faith. Make note of your questions since you will use them again in question 12.

Question 2. Use this question to survey the chapter.

Question 3. Think of specific tensions between "evil human desires" and the "will of God."

Question 4. Who are "those now dead" in verse 6? Are they the people Jesus preached to in 3:19? Or are they those who heard and received the gospel and later died? David H. Wheaton, writing in *The New Bible Commentary,* prefers the second choice, saying, "Those who have died (the dead) may be judged in the flesh like men, by suffering physical death, but, because the gospel was preached to them (while alive), when they responded, they are now living in the Spirit like God" (p. 1245). In other words, the living body is not all there is to life.

Question 6. Your group should find six instructions in this text. Note that Christians are to be "clear minded" and "self-controlled" (v. 7), "love each other deeply" (v. 8), "offer hospitality" (v. 9), use the gifts God gives them (v. 10), and speak and serve as representatives of God (v. 11).

Question 7. Notice specific reasons given for these practices in verses 7 and 8, as well as personal ideas about the practicality of these instructions.

Question 8. If you need a follow-up question here, ask, "How can you better join with these early Christians and perform your own works of service and teaching 'so that in all things God may be praised through Jesus Christ'?" (Consider your work in your occupation, home, church, community.)

Question 9. Find ten or more answers throughout these verses.

Question 10. Broaden the discussion at this point. Answers may come from the text or experience, from the early Christian era or today's.

Study 7. 1 Peter 5. TLC for Trying Times.
Purpose: To cultivate relationships with God and his people in a way that helps resist Satan during times of suffering.
Question 1. Use this question to survey the chapter.
Question 3. If you need background information, for your own benefit, on how the office of elder began in the early church, see Acts 14:23, 15:2 and 20:17.
Question 6. Notice that the text speaks of God, other believers and "your enemy the devil." All Christians must develop an appropriate response to each.
Question 7. Find about six instructions in these verses.
Question 8. The words *that* or *because* (or context that implies those words) give clues that a reason for the command comes next. Don't neglect verses 10 and 11.
Question 10. Use the entire chapter to think through an appropriate relationship with other Christians and with God himself. Consider also the expectation of opposition from Satan—and how you ought to respond to that. Notice ways in which a strengthened relationship with God and his people assists you in resisting your mutual enemy.
Question 11. Find about ten phrases that respond to this question. Verse 13 mentions "she who is in Babylon." Who is "she"? And where is Babylon? Explanations abound. Babylon may be (1) the ancient city in Mesopotamia by that name; (2) a Roman garrison town in Egypt now named Cairo; (3) Rome. "She" is likely to mean the church, but the word may also refer to Peter's wife mentioned in Mark 1:30 and in 1 Corinthians 9:5. *The New Bible Commentary* prefers the interpretation that the church in Rome sends her greetings to the readers of Peter's letter.

Study 8. 2 Peter 1:1-11. The Long Way Home.
Purpose: To promote a biblical balance of knowledge, faith and godly living.
Question 1. Find something that responds to this question in each verse from 3 to 11.
Question 2. Your group should find six or eight answers.
Question 3. Notice uses of the preposition *through* in verses 1-2.
Question 5. Be sure to treat both aspects of the question.
Question 6. Find four answers in verses 2-4.

Question 10. This question has plagued honest, Bible-believing Christians for centuries. Unless your group members all come from the same denomination they will likely differ in their interpretations of verse 10.

This division became apparent at the time of the Reformation. John Calvin agreed with Augustine that God gives his grace to some people (all of whom are totally sinful and unable to respond on their own), thereby calling and electing some to salvation. "For Calvin, predestination was a doctrine of comfort and assurance and should liberate the Christian from morbid introspection or debilitating insecurity" (Sinclair B. Ferguson and David F. Wright, eds., *New Dictionary of Theology* [Downers Grove, Ill.: InterVarsity Press, 1988], p. 527).

Jacobus Arminius, a Dutch Reformation theologian of the seventeenth century, disagreed. He said that since God knows all things, God knows who will choose to follow him. Therefore, "calling" and "election" refer to those whom God knows ahead of time will respond to him. John Wesley, and the many churches of his heritage, followed this interpretation.

A recent voice added to this debate is that of Karl Barth. Barth believed that Jesus Christ experienced both election and condemnation for all of humanity. (Information was gathered from the *New Dictionary of Theology*.)

Most Christians today interpret 2 Peter 1:10 with one of the biases cited above because we come from churches that grew from one of these theologians. With nearly two millennia of dispute as history to this question, a small group is not likely to solve the issue in ten minutes! Encourage discussion of possible meanings of the text. Generate respect for a variety of views, being sure that each one expressed does not conflict with information in the passage. Then move on to the final (and more practical) questions of the study.

Question 11. Refer to verses 5-9 for the effect on a person's life and verse 11 for the effect on the future. Draw on ideas found in your study throughout the passage as you try to incorporate them into your own individual goals.

Study 9. 2 Peter 1:12-21. If I Should Die . . .

Purpose: To live and share faith in a way that prepares for a satisfying death.

Question 3. Examine such phrases as "tent of this body," "put it aside," "my departure," "soon . . . as our Lord Jesus Christ has made clear to me."

Question 6. Using both the verses in 2 Peter and the verses in Matthew, you should find as many as eight or ten answers.

Question 7. In verse 16 Peter refers to the "cleverly invented stories" of many religious teachers. These were myths created to support heretical teachings. Peter deals with these teachings further in 2 Peter 2:1-3.

Question 9. Verse 19 is a difficult verse, subject to a variety of translations and interpretations. Troublesome phrases include the meanings of "more certain," "lamp," "dark," "the day," "morning star" and "in your hearts." The verse probably links several major concepts in Peter's letter: his description of Christ's majesty, his high view of the prophecy of Scripture and his hope of Christ's return, of which he speaks more fully in chapter 3.

The New Bible Commentary discusses this verse at length. Using its explanation of each phrase would result in an expanded translation similar to this: These happenings during the life of Jesus make it easier for us to believe the prophecies that he will come again. You should pay attention to them, because the Scripture is like a lamp shining in a world that is dark without the presence of Jesus. But Jesus will return. And that day will come like a dawn—with Jesus as the Morning Star who brings light and joy to your hearts.

Study 10. 2 Peter 2. Follow Which Leader?

Purpose: To recognize the dangers of false teaching.

Question 1. Use this question as a quick survey, not a thorough analysis. That will come as the study progresses.

Question 2. Find six or more answers in these verses. Notice particularly the words of verse 1: "denying the sovereign Lord who bought them."

The term "sovereign Lord" is used most often to name God. Here Peter uses it to name Christ, Peter's own assertion of Christ's deity. In pointing out that false teachers deny "the sovereign Lord who bought them," he also alerts his readers to a major warning sign of false teachings. Even today, cults almost always differ from the Christian faith in the area of the person and work of Jesus Christ.

Question 3. Find common elements in the three stories, then notice Peter's use of the words *if* and *then*. Be sure to notice the three-part summary beginning with the word *then* in verse 9.

Question 5. Find about twenty characteristics of false teachers in these verses.

Who was Balaam (mentioned in vv. 15-16)? This confusing story of Balaam appears in Numbers 22—24 and 31:1-16. Peter interprets Balaam's actions as selfish—an attempt to change God's message for personal profit. While Balaam seems relatively blameless in chapters 22—24 (except for some harsh discipline to his donkey), chapter 31 shows that he eventually joined the Midianite side—enemies of God's people.

Question 10. If you need a follow-up question, ask, "How are false teachers affected by their own falling away from faith?" "How are their followers affected?"

Several problems of interpretation arise out of verses 20-22. To whom is the warning addressed? The false teachers? Or those who may be deluded by their teachings? Scholars disagree. J. N. D. Kelly says that the warning refers to weak believers who are misled by false teaching. He believes that the verses emphasize the damage that false teachers can do to their followers. As supporting evidence, he adds that the words here agree with the strong warning of Hebrews 6:4-6 (*A Commentary on the Epistles of Peter and Jude*, Thornapple Commentaries [Grand Rapids, Mich.: Baker, 1969]).

But Michael Green (*The Second Epistle of Peter and the Epistle of Jude*, Tyndale New Testament Commentaries [Grand Rapids, Mich.: Eerdmans, 1968]) and David H. Wheaton (*New Bible Commentary*) take a different approach. They argue (with this author) that it is the false teachers themselves who are the object of this warning. As evidence, they note (1) that false teachers are the subject of the entire chapter and therefore this interpretation does not interrupt the flow of logic; (2) that verses 20-22 expand on the teachers' own bondage to corruption described in verse 19; (3) that verse 1 implies that the false teachers were once true believers so that they had indeed "escaped the corruption of the world by knowing our Lord," as verse 20 declares; (4) that the "sacred commandment" refers to Christ's Great Commission to his followers in Matthew 28:17-20, and that false teachers misuse and pervert this command.

Even so, the damage the teachers cause may well be the major thrust of the warning. Peter does not mention God's judgment on these teachers of falsehood or their eternal status. When Peter says, "It would have been better for them not to have known the way of righteousness," he may well have had in mind the close relationship to other believers that the initial belief of these false teachers provided—and the damage they caused because of that opportunity.

Study 11. 2 Peter 3. The Fire Next Time.
Purpose: To prepare for Christ's return.
Group discussion. To draw out group members you might also ask them how their work of art captures their thoughts and feelings about the end of the world.

Question 1. Survey the information in the passage. Notice that Peter connects his own message with the prophets of the Old Testament, with Christ's words and with the other apostles, including the apostle Paul. (In spite of a small jibe at Paul's inscrutability, Peter incidentally assigns the status of Scripture to Paul's letters.) Peter also mentions such goals as "wholesome thinking" in verse 1, as well as not being carried into error, not falling, growing instead in grace and knowledge of Jesus. Try to put yourself in the sandals of Peter's early readers and imagine what would have caught their attention—and why.

Question 4. Find information in verses 4-5 and 7.

Question 5. See verses 8-9 and 15. If you need a follow-up question, ask, "Why might this delay be considered an act of God's mercy?"

Verse 9 "has been cited as an argument for universalism: in fact it teaches the opposite. The plain thrust of it is that after the second coming, ushering in Christ's judgment, there will be no further opportunity for repentance, and so God in His mercy is giving men as long as possible to repent" (*New Bible Commentary,* p. 1257).

Question 7. Study each use of fire and water throughout the chapter.

Question 8. Find answers in verses 11, 12, 15, 17 and 18.

Question 11. If you are leading a group, don't expect anyone to answer all sections of this question and thus monopolize the conversation. Instead, encourage each person to respond to some aspect of it.

For additional New Testament descriptions of the end times, see Matthew 24; Mark 13; Luke 17:26-37; Acts 2:4-21; 1 Corinthians 15; 1 Thessalonians 4:13—5:5; Revelation 1:4-8; 20:11—22:21.

Study 12. Jude. The Twisted Fate of Twisted Faith.

Purpose: To become alert to perversions of the Christian life and faith.

Question 2. Find a half dozen or more answers in these verses. Who were James and Jude? Both Matthew 13:55 and Mark 6:3 speak of them (along with Joseph and Simon) as brothers of Jesus. Though, according to John 7:5, Christ's brothers were not believers in him during his lifetime, these two at least became converts after his death.

James became a leader in the early church. We see him in action in Acts 12:17, 15:13 and 21:18; 1 Corinthians 15:7; Galatians 1:19 and 2:9, 12. We hear from Jude only in this book, except perhaps in 1 Corinthians 9:5. It is interesting to note that while Jude claims James as brother, both he and James refer to themselves as servants of Jesus.

Question 4. Find as many as sixteen items in verses 4, 8-10, 16 and 19. If you study the metaphors of verses 12-13, you will find six more characteristics—but you will treat these six more thoroughly in question 9.

Question 7. Help your group examine each word in the title. As your group discusses this confession about Jesus, you should come to conclusions similar to the following definitions: *Jesus:* the historical person who was born, lived and died in Palestine. *Christ:* Messiah promised as a redeemer to the Jews through the Old Testament. *Our:* defines a sense of belonging—he is ours; we know, love and serve him. *Only:* no other being in heaven or on earth qualifies for this position. *Sovereign:* Jesus rules all of heaven and earth, its peoples and beings, its past, present and future. *Lord:* He is my master. I serve him and give him all that I have and all that I am. I do his will. I allow him to rule me.

Question 8. Don't spend undue discussion time on these characters. Simply gather the gist of why Jude refers to them and move on. These characters appear in various parts of the Old Testament and in several Jewish apocryphal books. For further study you may consult the following: Jewish release from Egypt (Ex 12:31—14:31); fallen angels (Gen 6:1-4 and several apocryphal books); Sodom and Gomorrah (Gen 18—19); Michael and Moses (The Assumption of Moses—an apocryphal book); Cain (Gen 4:1-16); Balaam (Num 22—24); Korah (Num 16); Enoch (Gen 5:1-18 and the apocryphal book of Enoch).

Question 10. Your group should list and then discuss the ways Jude advises us to build ourselves up. We are to pray in the Holy Spirit (v. 20), to keep ourselves in God's love (v. 21), to be merciful to those who doubt (v. 22), to snatch people from the fire (v. 23) and to show mercy mixed with fear (v. 23).

Linger as long as necessary on the second half of this question. You will need its thoughtful consideration to answer question 13.

Question 13. Your previous discussion of questions 7, 10 and 11 should provide background for the more personal answers to this question.

Carolyn Nystrom is a freelance writer living in St. Charles, Illinois. She has written more than seventy Bible study guides and books for adults and children.

ALSO FOR SMALL GROUPS

As well as over 70 titles in the popular Lifebuilder series, Scripture Union produces a wide variety of resources for small groups. Among them are:

❖ **The Word made fresh!** – a series of A4 discussion starters based on relevant contemporary teaching from internationally-known preacher Stephen Gaukroger; ten sessions with worksheets in each.

❖ **Connect Bible Studies** – a range based on contemporary issues, looking at what biblical principles we might apply to understanding them.

❖ **Deeper Encounter** – for confident groups having a good understanding of Bible text, seven studies complete with CD audio tracks and photocopiable worksheets.

❖ **Small Groups Growing Churches** – a flexible training resource for leading small groups. Can be used as a complete 15-topic training course, for a tailor-made church weekend, or for one-off refresher sessions.

❖ **Essential 100** and **Essential Jesus** – 100-reading overview of the Bible (*Essential 100*) and the person of Jesus (*Essential Jesus*), with notes and helps presented as a programme for individuals or small groups.

❖ **The Multi-Sensory series** – resources for creative small groups, youth groups and churches, to appeal to a wide range of learning styles.

SU also has a range of Lent studies, plus a free online magazine for small groups called church@home. Go to www.scriptureunion.org.uk/churchathome

SU publications are available from Christian bookshops, on the Internet, or via mail order. Advice on what would suit your group best is always available. You can:

- phone SU's mail order line: local rate number 08450 706006
- email info@scriptureunion.org.uk
- log on to www.scriptureunion.org.uk
- write to SU Mail Order, PO Box 5148, Milton Keynes MLO, MK2 2YX

ipture Union
IG THE BIBLE TO INSPIRE CHILDREN, YOUNG PEOPLE AND
TS TO KNOW GOD